For Vivian French, with love — S. P.

For Jack and Penny — A. J.

Henry Holt and Company, LLC
Publishers since 1866
115 West 18th Street
New York, New York 10011

First published in the United States in 2001 by Henry Holt and Company, LLC.
Published in Canada by Fitzhenry & Whiteside Ltd., 195 Allstate Parkway, Markham, Ontario L3R 4T8.
Originally published in Great Britain in 2001 by Frances Lincoln Limited.

Library of Congress Card Number: 00-109999

ISBN 0-8050-6783-3
First American Edition—2001
Printed in Singapore
1 3 5 7 9 10 8 6 4 2

A Ladder to the Stars

Simon Puttock

Illustrated by Alison Jay

Henry Holt and Company

New York

It was a little girl's birthday. She was seven years old. From her bedroom window she looked out and saw a single star dancing in the velvet blue. It glittered and spun so beautifully she wished she could climb right up into the sky and dance along with it.

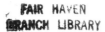

E
PUTTOCK

"Twinkle, twinkle, little star.
How I wonder what you are!
I wish I may, I wish I might,
have the wish I wish tonight."

The star heard the little girl and began to show off, whirling
and dipping as never before.

When the moon rose, it saw the star capering and was curious.

"What are you doing, little star?"

The star turned cartwheels and told the moon about the little
girl's wish.

The moon grew round and full pondering the matter, then wasted away to a splinter worrying about what to do.

"I must tell the sun," the moon decided, "for the sun is also a star and loves all things that love to dance."

The sun called the wind and the clouds and the weather together, and they thought up a plan.

The wind set out to find a special seed. It whistled away to
billow and blow through every nook and cranny of the planet.

At last, worn down to the breath of a breeze, the wind found the special seed and blew it gently to the little girl's garden and planted it in a dusty corner.

Soon the seed sent a root into the soil. It pushed up
a slender stem and spread leaves to the light of the
waiting sun.

It grew . . .

and grew . . .

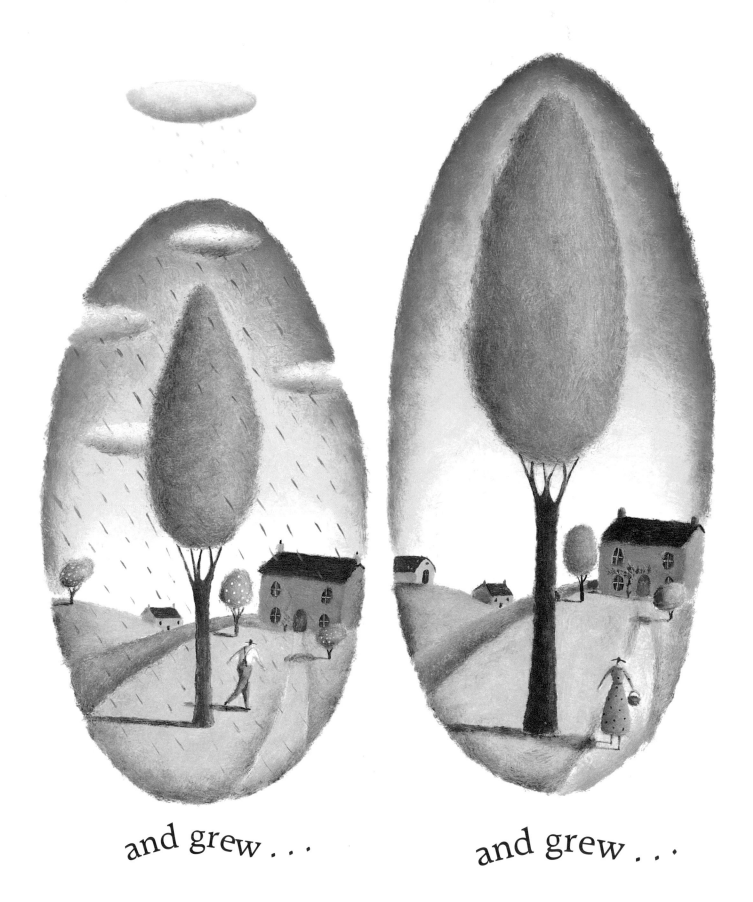

and grew . . .   and grew . . .

and did not stop growing until . . .

. . . one day it had grown so high, the tips of its branches brushed the belly of the sky.

When the leaves tickled the sun as it passed overhead,
the sun told the moon to tell the star to tell the little girl
that her wish had been granted.

It was an old woman's birthday. She
was one hundred and seven years old.
That night when she went to bed,
she lay counting the stars like distant
friends in the frame of her window.

But a single piercing beam of starlight shone in
and would not let her sleep.

"Hey, little girl!"
The old woman rubbed her eyes and looked up at the sky.
"Who, me?"
"Yes, you," said the star.
"I'm not a little girl. I'm an old woman, and I'm tired.
Now go away and let me sleep."
"Come out and climb the tree. Come up and dance,"
the star entreated. "It was your wish."

"Are you crazy?" cried the old woman. "That must have been a hundred years ago. I am too old and it is too late now to climb to the top of that great, tall tree."

"It is never too late," said the star. "Why, one hundred years are nothing and no time. To a star, they are light and quick like seeds in the wind. You are still a little girl to us, and we are waiting for you. Please come."

The old woman, whose life had been long and whose bones were weary, remembered how it felt to be young and carefree. She remembered, too, a birthday long ago when the sky had seemed vast and mysterious. Above her the stars winked and beckoned.

"I will," she said at last. "I WILL!"

And despite her aching back and trembling limbs, she fetched
a chair to stand on, rubbed her hands on the bark for luck,
and began to climb.

It was breathless, hot, hard work. The old woman felt
inclined to grumble as she climbed. Below her the city lights
sparkled like another sky of stars.

"Twinkle, twinkle, silly star.
How I wish you weren't so far!"

But as she climbed higher, the air grew cooler and clearer
and the climbing easier, until she was so high up that
the world was lost in the clouds beneath her feet.
She was climbing so fast that when
she reached the top she bumped
her head hard against the
belly of midnight.
"Ouch!"

She rubbed her head and eyed the sky an inch above
her nose, as branches swayed beneath her feet.
"Good-bye, good-bye," she told the tree.
"All those years I sat in your shade
and watched you grow,
but I never knew
you grew for me.
Thank you."

Then she spat on her hands for strength, and with a mighty effort pushed and pulled and wriggled and heaved her way though the satin skin of the sky.

"Oh my! Oh my! How elegant you are," she said to the stars. "You twinkle like diamonds."

"Thank you," said her special star. "Shall we dance at last?"
The old woman smiled and held out her hands, and they kicked
up their heels till a million sparks like newborn comets flew,
and off they spun across the endless velvet blue.

All this was a long, long time ago, but when you
are dancing with stars, the years are little and quick
like seeds in the wind.

She is dancing still.